© Copyright 2019 - Dinobibi: All rights reserved. No part of this publication may be reproduced, stored in retrieval systems, or transmitted by any means, including electronic, mechanical, photocopying, or otherwise, without prior written permission of the publisher and copyright holder. **Disclaimer:** Although the author and Dinobibi have taken all reasonable care in preparing this book, we make no warranty about the accuracy or completeness of its content and, to the maximum extent permitted, disclaim all liability arising from its use.

CONTENTS

Introduction (pg. 4)

Geography of South Korea (pg. 7)

Weather (pg. 16)

History (pg. 21)

Culture and Traditions (pg. 25)

Native Planst & Animals (pg. 30)

Famous People (pg. 35)

Major Cities & Attractions (pg. 39)

INTRODUCTION: HELLO FRIENDS!

Hi friends! Welcome to South Korea! My name is Chang. I am a 12-year-old boy living with my parents in Seoul, the capital of South Korea. I'm so excited to take you to a tour to my beautiful country!

I have a little sister, Ji-woo, and she is 10 years old. Both of us work hard at our public school.

My father is an electronics engineer and my mother teaches English in a primary school.

Fun Facts about Korean Schools:

Teachers are like gods for us students. They are highly respected in our society. Most teachers wear suits or blazers to school. We like our teachers looking smart and modern.

Classrooms are well equipped with computers and other devices that helps with our learning.

We take responsibility for the cleanliness of our classrooms and the entire school. We clean our classroom by taking turns every morning before the school bell rings.

Nearly 95% of the people in my country are literate.

Before we start our tour, I would like to know more about you.
Can you please complete this little questionnaire for me?

Your name:

Which country are you from:

Who are you traveling with?

Which places in South Korea are you most exicited about? Why?

Korea became independent in 1945, but was broken into two countries: North Korea and South Korea. Just to clarify, I am from South Korea. However, for most Koreans, our country remains a single nation and cannot really be divided.

The official name of South Korea is the Republic of Korea, and is also known as the 'Land of the Morning Calm.' This name is believed to have been taken from the word 'Choson' (one of the important dynasties to have ruled over Korea). 'Cho' translates to 'morning' and 'son' means light or bright. Therefore, 'bright morning' is the English translation of 'Choson' and the nickname, the 'Land of the Morning Calm' has come from this.

CHAPTER 1
GEOGRAPHY OF SOUTH KOREA

South Korea, as the name suggests, is situated on the southern side of the Korean Peninsula. The Korean Peninsula is 1200 km (750 miles) long. South Korea's total area is about 98500 square kilometers (about 38000 square miles). This beautiful country of mine is home to many hills and mountains with broad coastal plains in the southern and western side. However, many of our hills and peaks are millions of years old, and they have been worn down by wind and water.

Many of the peaks in South Korea are less than 1,000 m (3300 feet) high. South Korea is bordered by North Korea in the north, the Yellow Sea in the west, the East China Sea in the southwest, the East Sea, also called the Sea of Japan, in the northeast.

Jeju Island

The tropical evergreen forests can be found on Jeju Island along a narrow strip of land in the south. And thanks to heavy rainfall and high humidity in South Korea, nearly 50% of South Korea is covered in forests.

What is a Peninsula?

1. A piece of land bordered by water on two sides.
2. A piece of land that has water on three sides.
3. Land surrounded by water.

Answer: (1) It is a piece of land that has water on three sides.

There are nine provinces (or states) in South Korea. We will skip learning the names of all of them because they can sound complex to a foreign kid who does not know the Korean language.

I will just tell you that Seoul, the capital of South Korea, is located in the Gyeonggi Province, which is the largest and most populous state in my country.

The official language of South Korea is Korean. Language experts believe that the Korean language is closely related to Mongolian, Turkish, and Japanese languages.

The Korean alphabet was created by King Sejong the Great of Joseon in 1446 We even have a special day to celebrate the Korean alphabet called Hangul Day.

Public Statue of King Sejong, The Great King

Important Rivers of South Korea

My country is a leading exporter of robotics, automobiles, and electronics, and the rivers play a big part in the economy of South Korea. Let me tell you about some of the most important rivers here.

Han River — The Han River is the fourth largest river in South Korea, and one part of it rises in Mount Geumgang in North Korea. The Han River passes through the capital city, Seoul and then joins the Imjin River to finally flow into the Yellow Sea.

The total length of the Han River is 514 km (about 319 miles). Today, the Han River is not used for navigation because of the various issues that still exist between North and South Korea. You can find many sports facilities and parks along the banks of the Han River. There are river cruises on this beautiful river that allow you to take in the magical scenery of Seoul's waterfront areas.

There are 27 bridges on the Han River connecting the northern and southern parts of Seoul.

Nakdong River — This is the longest river in South Korea, and it flows through important cities including Busan and Daegu. It originates in the Taebaek Mountains and flows into the Korean Strait.

Imjin River — There is a demilitarized zone between North and South Korea, which you can read more about the 'History of South Korea' chapter. The interesting thing about the Imjin River is that it flows through this demilitarized zone.

At certain points along the bank of the Imjin River, there are vertical cliffs that are as high as 75 feet. At certain points along the bank of the Imjin River, there are vertical cliffs that are as high as 75 feet.

Geumgang River — It originates in the North Jeolla Province and flows into the Yellow Sea.

Islands of South Korea

Jejudo Island is a UNESCO World Heritage Site, meaning it is marked as an important place that needs to be preserved and protected because it holds many ancient and natural marvels.

There are more than 3300 islands off the coast of South Korea. That means, if you visited one island a day, it would take you more than nine years to see all of them! The most important and the largest one is Jejudo Island.

UNESCO is a global organization (part of the United Nations) that works to preserve ancient monuments, buildings, and treasures of the world.

Jejudo Islands has one of the best lava tube caves system in the world. These caves were formed naturally by flowing lava. The tubes drain out all the lava during a volcanic eruption. When the flow of lava stops, the rocks cool down and become hard leaving behind a long tube cave!

Can you guess the nickname of Jejudo Islands?

1. The Lava Island
2. The Venice of the East
3. The Hawaii of Korea

Answer: (3) The Hawaii of Korea

Mountains of South Korea

Hills and mountains take up nearly 70% of the landscape in South Korea. There are three major mountain ranges in my country, and they are:

- Taebaek Mountains
- Sobaek Mountains
- The Jiri Massif

The Taebak Mountains – This mountain range is located on the eastern edge of South Korea. The important mountain peaks in this range are Mount Seoraksan, Mount Kumgangsan, and Mount Taebaeksan. The eastern side of this mountain range falls steeply into the sea, while the western side has gentler slopes. Both the Han River and the Nakdong River start from Taebaek Mountain Range.

The Sobaek Mountains — This mountain range split off from the Taebaek Mountain Range and cuts right across the center of the Korean Peninsula. It extends towards the southwestern part of the country. The highest mountain peak here is Jirisan.

The Jiri Massif — Also known locally as Jirisan, this mountain range forms the southern part of the Sobaek Mountains and is considered to be a highly sacred and spiritual place. It is the second highest peak in my country, and seven Buddhist temples are located here.

Hwaeomsa Temple, literally "Flower Garland Temple", is one of the ancient Bhuddist temples in Jirisan National Park.

THe Halla Mountains or "Hallasan" during winter.

The Halla Mountains — It is the tallest peak in South Korea and is located on the Jejudo Island. The Hallasan Natural Reserve which is a natural monument to South Korea, is also located here.

View of Baengnokdam, at the peak of Hallasan.

Halla Mountain is a dormant (sleeping) volcano, and its peak is a crater lake, called Baengnokdam, literally meaning "white deer lake"

Hallasan is home to Gwaneumsa, the oldest Buddhist temple on Jeju Island. It is one of the most visited places on the island.

Flag of South Korea

The flag of South Korea is called Taegukgi or Taegeukgi which means the 'Supreme Ultimate Flag.' The need for a separate Korean flag was felt in the late 19th century when external forces started invading Korea, but the flag of my country wasn't officially adopted until January 25, 1950.

It was designed by Park Yeong-Hyo, a political leader of the late 19th century.

Traditional signs and symbols were used to form the flag. The rectangular flag has a white background with a red and blue taegeuk in the center and four black trigrams at the corners.

The taegeuk is a figure with two red and blue interlocking semicircles. One of the semicircles represents the positive elements of the world, and the other one represents the negative elements. Therefore, the taegeuk represents the balance or the yin-yang of the universe. The black trigrams represent movement (or progress) and harmony.

Can you guess what the white color in our flag means?

1. Equality
2. Cleanliness
3. Peace and purity

Answer: (3) Peace and purity

Other National Symbols

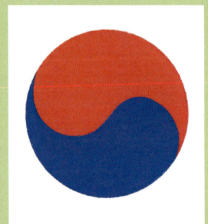

The taegeuk is the **national emblem** of my country and it's used in government seals and stamps.

Our **national tree** is the Korean red pine, locally called "sonamu". It is considered to represent Korean spirit and is even mentioned in the South Korean national anthem, Aegukga.

Our **national bird** is the Korean magpie, and our **national animal** is the Siberian tiger.

Can you guess the national sport of South Korea?

1. Football
2. Tennis
3. Tae Kwon Do

Answer: (3) Tae Kwon Do

The **national flower** of South Korea is mugunghwa which is also called the Rose of Sharon.

Mugunghwa translates to 'eternal bloom that never fades.' Also, for the Koreans, this flower represents the balance in the entire universe.

Currency

The currency of my country is the South Korean won. The smallest unit of currency in South Korea is jeon but it's rarely used so, the smallest usable money is 1 won. To give you an idea, here is a small list of common things we use every day along with the cost.

1 liter of milk — 2400₩
A loaf of white bread - 2900₩
A kilogram of rice - 4150₩
A pair of name-brand jeans - 66000₩

CHAPTER 2
WEATHER IN SOUTH KOREA

South Korea climate is temperate and has four distinct seasons. Any time of the year is good to visit South Korea. However, each season offers different experiences for travelers, and you can choose the time to come and see my country depending on what you want to see and experience. Let me give you a small idea of each of the four seasons and the important holidays and festivals.

Spring

Spring in South Korea is between April and June. The cherry blossom trees are in full bloom during this time, and the entire country looks like it is painted pink, which is a beautiful sight to see. The weather is very pleasant during spring with temperatures at tolerable levels. Many visitors like to come here during spring, so it is the most crowded time of the year.

The start of spring can be seen by mid-March itself when Jeju Island comes alive in yellow colors; the color of the rapeseed flower. Then, the pink cherry blossoms, bright yellow flowers of the forsythia, and many more blossoms bloom converting the landscape into a riot of colors.

National Holidays in Spring

Hanging Lanterns for Buddha's Birthday

Some of holidays and festivals that we celebrate in spring are:

March 1 — Also called the March First Movement, this holiday commemorates the day when we first started fighting for freedom from Japanese occupancy, which started on March 1, 1919.

April 5 — This holiday is celebrated every year as Arbor Day to promote tree-planting. Groups and individuals come out together to plant trees and celebrate the power and beauty of nature.

May 5 — Children's Day in South Korea, observed since 1922, is celebrated on May 5th. Started by a children's book writer, Bang Jeong-hwan, he told all adults to treat children with love and respect. On this day, my parents (and nearly all parents in the country) take their children out for a fun day!

Buddha's birthday — Buddha's birthday is celebrated every year according to the Chinese lunar calendar. So, the dates keep changing each year and usually fall between late April and early June.

On this day, most Koreans visit Buddhist temples and honor Buddha. People carry rice and other offerings to give to Buddhist monks during their temple visit.

What is the name of the religion that Buddha founded?

1. Christianity
2. Hinduism
3. Buddhism

(Answer – 3. Buddhism)

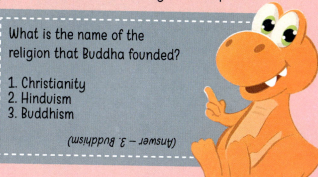

Summer

The summer season is between July and August. The days are quite warm. But, we get to experience the monsoon, or heavy, rains in July and August. Most people tend to avoid visiting Korea during this time because the constant rains can dampen your travel plans.

The summer months are best for visiting great beaches. Water sports such as windsurfing, water skiing, diving, and rafting are available in different places along the banks of the Han River. Of course, you must be prepared for the high humidity and heavy rainfall during this season.

National Holidays in Summer

Some of the national holidays in the summer months are:

June 6 — On this Memorial Day, we remember and honor the soldiers (both men and women) who died in different battles and wars including the Korean War. Most places across the country are closed on this important day.

July 17 - The Constitution Day is celebrated every year on July 17th. On this day, in 1948, the Constitution of the Republic of Korea was officially adopted.

Sadly, this day was also the day when North and South Korea were separated. So, some people don't like to remember this day because they were separated from their loved ones who lived on the other side of the 38th Parallel (the line that divides North and South Korea).

Autumn

Maple trees with a lake at Gyeongbokgung Palace

When the rains stop, my country looks stunning because the autumn leaves begin changing their colors to beautiful shades of orange and red. Autumn is as beautiful as spring in South Korea with mild temperatures, very little rainfall, and an abundance of natural beauty with blooming flowers and the changing colors of the autumn leaves.

Autumn in South Korea is invigorating and beautiful. We have pure blue skies, and the temperatures are wonderfully comfortable. As autumn is the time of harvest, many traditional festivals and customs are practiced during this time.

When do you think is the autumn season in South Korea?

1. January-March
2. March-April
3. September-November

Answer: (3) September-November

National Holidays in Autumn

Some of the important holidays celebrated and observed during the autumn season are:

Thanksgiving — Thanksgiving in South Korea is celebrated on the 15th day of the 8th month of the Chinese lunar calendar. Usually, it comes around mid-September.

Chuseok is an important harvest festival which is also called Hangawai, meaning, 'Autumn Eve.'

Gaecheonjeol or National Foundation Day is celebrated on the third of October. This day commemorates the formation of Gojoseon, the first Korean state.

Korean Alphabet Day, October 9 is Hangeul Day in my country. This day is to honor and celebrate the invention of the modern writing system of the Korean language.

Winter

Deogyusan mountains is covered by snow and morning fog in winter

Winter in Korea is between December and March. With snow all over the country, it is a lovely time to visit Korea. Yes, it might be cold and snowy, but rainfall is rare during winter.

But, with the right clothing, you can have a great time here because most places will not be very crowded. And our transportation system works like clockwork even during the cold winter months. Don't be scared of the cold. Go ahead and plan your winter holiday in South Korea.

National Holidays in Winter

Here are some of my favorite winter holidays:

Christmas - Like the rest of the world, South Korea celebrates Christmas Day on December 25.

New Year - We celebrate two New Year's day in my country. The first one is on January 1 like the rest of the wold, and the second one is called "Seollal" or Korean New Year which is celebrated on the first day of the first month of the lunar calendar.

CHAPTER 3
HISTORY OF SOUTH KOREA

Archeological evidence shows that people have been living in South Korea for at least 10,000 years. Experts believe that the original inhabitants of my country might have come from Siberia and Mongolia.

By 4000 B.C., the people living in Korea were Stone Age farmers, and by 1000 B.C. they had learned to use bronze, too. By 300 B.C., Koreans started making weapons and tools of iron. Initially, Korea had many tribes, which later on combined to form big and powerful kingdoms.

The first kingdom of Korea is the Old Chosun Kingdom. The rulers of this kingdom ruled over the northern parts of Korea and also controlled some parts of China for nearly 22 centuries.

In 108 B.C., the Old Chosun Empire was overthrown by the Chinese. From then until 688 A.D., the entire area of present-day Korea was divided into and controlled by three different kingdoms including Pekche, Shilla, and Koguryo. Koguryo was in the northern part of undivided Korea, and Pekche and Shilla controlled the southern parts.

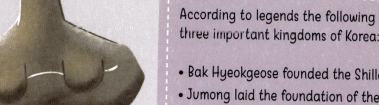

According to legends the following people founded each of these three important kingdoms of Korea:

- Bak Hyeokgeose founded the Shilla Kingdom in 57 B.C.
- Jumong laid the foundation of the Koguryo Kingdom in 37 B.C.
- Onjo founded the Pekche Kingdom in 18 B.C.

By the 4th century, Korea was a highly civilized nation. In 688 A.D., the Shilla Kingdom unified the area into one nation and ruled over it until 935 A.D. The Shilla rulers were helped by the Chinese.

Korea under the Shilla Rule

Even when Korea was unified under one kingdom, it was still a mixture of many tribes. A council of tribal leaders, called the hwabaek, advised the king and also had the power to choose the next king.

Korea, in those times, was strictly hierarchical, which means people belonged to different levels of society depending on the work they did and how important they were.

Who do you think had the highest social rank in the Korean society?

1. The hwabaek
2. The King
3. The common people

Answer: (2) It's the king!

The nobles were also divided into different ranks based on their importance. Most of the Koreans were serfs who were primarily farmers and traders. Korea built a university under the Shilla Rule where Confucianism was taught. However, only nobles were admitted to this university. The common people were not allowed entry.

Buddhism came to Korea in the 4th century, and many Buddhist temples were constructed all over the country. By the end of the 8th century, the Shilla Kingdom disintegrated because there were fights as to who would become king.

Seokguram Grotto from the Silla era

Korea under the Koryo Rule

Toward the end of the Shilla Rule, many of the tribal leaders broke away and formed their own kingdoms. One such powerful tribal leader was Taejo Wang Geon who founded the Koryo Kingdom.

The Koryo Kingdom, which came after the Shilla Kingdom, lasted from 935 A.D. until 1392 A.D. Now, can you guess how Korea got its name? Yes, you are right. As you may have guessed, my country is named after the Koryo Kingdom.

One of the biggest challenges the Koryo Kingdom faced was from the Mongols who destroyed many parts of the mainland. They conquered Koryo and its rulers became their pawns.

Korea under the Choson Rule

In 1392, the Choson Dynasty, formed by the Yi family, came to power and ruled over Korea until 1910 when Japan annexed the country.

The society during the Choson Rule was called the 'yangban' society. The 'yangban' was a special section of scholars and military officials who controlled most parts of the society during that time.

> During the Choson dynasty, the capital was moved to Hanseong which is now the modern day Seoul.
>
> It was during this period that Korea saw a lot of advancement in science and education.
>
> The Korean alphabet or "Hangul" was also developed during this time in order to educate common people.

Although the Choson Dynasty ruled over Korea until 1910, larger countries on the Asian continent invaded and controlled Korea.

Japan invaded us in the 1500s. And in the 1900s, both Russia and China invaded and tried to take Korea from Japanese control. However, Japan was able to fend off both the Russian and Chinese attacks and annexed, or joined, Korea.

In 1894, China and Japan sent soldiers to suppress a rebellion in Korea. From then on, China, Japan, and Russia continuously battled with each other to keep control of Korea. Japan defeated China and Russia and took control of Korea in 1910.

North and South Korea

In World War II, Japan was defeated, and when they surrendered to the US, Korea was split into two entities named North and South Korea. North Korea was under the control of Russia and South Korea was under the control of the US.

In 1950, North Korea invaded South Korea, and the Korean War began which lasted for three years until 1953, which was the time of the Cold War when Russia and the US were not really fighting with each other directly. However, they were 'cold' towards each other and not on friendly terms.

Now, recall that North Korea was controlled by Russia and South Korea by the US. So, the Korean War was actually an indirect result of the Cold War between the US and Russia.

South Korea eventually regained control over its territories, and the Korean War did appear to end. However, no peace agreement was ever signed and even today, there is a demilitarized region at the border of North and South Korea where neither sides can place military camps.

Independence of South Korea

Remember that Korea was invaded and controlled by the Japanese for a long time and has built bridges, roads, factories, and railways all across Korea during their rule. A lot of cities were also established in this time but the Koreans wanted freedom from the Japanese government, so they held peaceful protests and marches asking the Japanese to leave Korea. Korea finally gained independence after World War II.

On August 15, 1948, the independent government that we know today was created, and Syngman Rhee, the first South Korean President was elected in office. On the following year, the date was officially designated as a public holiday called **Gwangbokjeol,** literally meaning "the day the light returned".

During Gwangbokjeol, houses and building are encouraged to display the South Korean national flag. Some places and public transports are also free of charge to the descendants of independence activists on the holiday.

Present Day South Korea

Today, a presidential system of government is in place. Like the US, the president of South Korea is elected by the people, and he (or she) is supported by the executive, legislature, and the judiciary branches in running the government.

The legislative branch of the South Korean government has more than 270 members who are also elected by the people of my country every four years. The judiciary branch is made up of judges, lawyers, high courts, the Supreme Court, and the smaller courts too.

Our economy has also grown a lot and South Korea has become one of the leaders in different industries including telecommunications, steel, and electronics.

Can you guess which one of these companies is from South Korea?

1. Toyota
2. Samsung
3. Sony

Answer: (2) Samsung

CHAPTER 4
CULTURE & TRADITONS OF SOUTH KOREA

The primary religions followed in Korea are Confucianism, Buddhism, and Christianity. The Constitution of South Korea supports religious freedom, so you can follow any religion in my country although most Koreans believe in and follow the rituals of Confucianism even today.

Confucianism

Confucianism was founded by Confucius, a highly educated Chinese man who lived in the 4th – 5th century B.C. He set rules and regulations for people to follow so that nobody behaves in any wrong way. He deeply believed in people respecting each other, and everyone respecting the ruler. He believed and preached good moral conduct.

He set up a code of behavior for all his followers to lead a good, moral life. The two main cultural festivals in Korea are the Chuseok (or Thanksgiving) and Seollal (the local new year as the lunar calendar). On these two days, celebrations are based around family, ancestors, food, harvest, etc.

The Family

The family plays an integral role in the society and culture of South Korea. All traditions and customs are based on the concept of family. The eldest son in every family has more responsibility than the other children.

In a traditional korean family, much of the responsibility is placed on the males.

The Koreans believe that the eldest son has to look after the parents when they are old.

Each person in a korean family has a clearly defined role and functions interdependently with the other family members.

Chuseok

Chuseok is the Korean Thanksgiving Day, and on this day, we connect with our roots. Most of us travel to our original hometowns to honor our ancestors.

In the house, all family members eat together on this day, and a variety of foods are served including fish, meats, vegetables, fruits, dumplings, sweet rice, and many more.

The foods are all neatly and beautifully arranged near the family shrine. We believe that these offerings are for our ancestors, and they can enjoy the feast if it is delicious and also presented well to them.

This dish is made with rice flour and has a sweet filling made of beans, sesame, and chestnuts, then steamed and served hot.

Traditional women's hanbok consists of an upper garment called jeogori, and a high-waist skirt called chima. Men's hanbok consists of a jacket called jeogori and loose-fitting baji or trousers. They're colorful and comfortable to wear so many tourist even rent one when visiting temples.

The most traditional food connected to Chuseok is songpyeon, a delicious sweet dish. We children love songpyeon. When my mom makes it at home, the whole house smells of pine because they are steamed on pine needles.

In Korea, Chuseok is not just for giving thanks but also for fun and happiness. We kids wear the beautiful, silk hanbok, and there is a lot of singing and dancing. I have to tell you about one particularly interesting story behind the origins ganggangsullae, a dance in which women join and move in a circle.

In 1592, when the Japanese attacked Korea, the Korean general wanted to trick the enemy into thinking that we had a large military force. So, he made the women dress as men and dance in a circle. I am not sure if this story is true, but, it is very interesting, isn't it?

Seollal

This event is the lunar New Year celebrated with great pomp in Korea. Again, spending time with the family is the most important thing. All family members gather together in one home and enjoying a delicious meal.

Tteokguk is a traditional Korean rice cake soup served with vegetables and meat that is a must-try during this festive season. We believe drinking one bowl of tteokguk makes us one year older. So, we kids try to drink as many bowls as we can! Family games are played all day long.

Other Important Traditions of South Korea

Shoes off — Before you enter a Korean home, you must remove your footwear and leave them at the designated place. We have a deep connection with the floor. We eat, sleep, and sit on it. Walking with your shoes inside the house is considered rude.

Hiking — We love to hike. And it is natural, considering that a large part of our country is covered with mountains. Also, many of the mountains are not very high either, and hiking is considered the national pastime of Korea.

Blood type — Koreans believe that our blood type decides our personality. For example, a person with blood type B is considered to be more social and outgoing than people with other blood types.

Mandatory military service — All the men in South Korea are required to do military service for 21 – 24 months. This is mandatory which means South Korean men don't have a choice.

Confusing birthdays — Koreans believe that when we are born we are already one year old (because we have spent 9 months in our mother's wombs). This can cause some confusion when talking about age, especially when talking to Westerners. So, for example, if a Korean says he is 9 years old, then it means he is only 8 years old.

Seaweed soup for birthdays - The traditional birthday dish in Korea is the seaweed soup.

The unlucky number 4 — We Koreans believe that the number 4 is an unlucky number. So, many hotels and buildings do not have 4th floors!

Nabichum — Called as the butterfly dance, Nabichum is one of the most easily recognized Korean Buddhist dances an is a dance performed for various Buddhist rituals.

Popular Korean Foods

Can you guess the most favorite dish in Korea?
1. Kimchi
2. Tteokguk
3. Songpyeon

Answer: (1) Kimchi

In fact, **kimchi** is not just food, but is is a culture in Korea. Kimchi is nothing but sliced pickled cabbage, anchovy paste, and red chili sauce. It is sour, spicy, and delicious.

You will find kimchi on the table at every meal. Not only is it the most favorite side dish in the country, but is also the national dish of South Korea.

Rice is the staple food in my country. It is paired with different kinds of stews, curries, and of course, kimchi. Rice cultivation was started way back in the 3rd century.

Bulgogi — This dish seems to have been in existence since 37 B.C. as part of the Korean diet. Made of thin slices of meat marinated with a sweet or spicy sauce, and is then grilled, broiled, or stir-fried. Typically, we take a bit of bulgogi on a lettuce leaf, add a little sauce, wrap, and eat it up.

Japchae — This dish is sweet potato noodles stir-fried in sesame oil and is served with vegetables or beef.

Bindae-tteok — These are yummy pancakes made with mung beans and vegetables. They are crispy and absolutely delicious.

Mandu — These Korean-style dumplings are stuffed with beef, pork, or any other meat. If you like, you can use vegetable fillings too.

Pajeon — Also called Korean scallion pancakes, this dish is crispy on the outside and soft on the inside. You can eat it as a main dish, a starter, or a side dish, too.

Korean rice cakes — Made with rice powder and pumpkin, Korean rice cakes are chewy and soft and usually eaten with tea.

Gogi-gui — or 'meat roast' is a method of grilling meat with gas or charcoal. This dish has also become popular worldwide as Korean Barbecue as it allows people commune while cook their own meal.

Kongguksu — Also, a noodle dish, it is served in cold soy-bean soup.

Samgyeop-sal — literally means "three layer flesh," or "pork belly", is a cut of meat that is also often found in korean grills along with a variety of side dishes and sauces like kimchi, korean coleslaw, cucumber salad and much more!

CHAPTER 5
NATIVE PLANTS AND ANIMALS

South Korea is home to a large number of animal and plant species. Let us look at a few of them:

White-naped crane – These beautiful, large birds can easily be identified by their white napes (the back of their necks).

The white-naped cranes have distinctive red patches around their eyes. Many of the species migrate to South Korea in the winters. They live in the marshy lands in the dematerialized zone (DMZ).

Just to help you recall, the DMZ is the non-military zone between North and South Korea. Some of the cranes move on to southern Japan to spend their winters.

Lynx – These are beautiful, thick-furred cats that live alone. The toes of these cats are naturally designed to work like snowshoes, making it easy for them to move around in the snow. They are found in the forest areas of the DMZ. They hunt at night, they avoid human beings, and it is not easy to catch sight of them.

Can you guess why they have such thick furs?
1. To look beautiful
2. To help humans get beautiful fur
3. To keep them warm during cold winters

Answer: (3) To keep them warm during cold winters

Asiatic black bear — With a soft, smooth, black coat, these huge bears have a white V-shaped patch on their chest. They are one of the most endangered species of mammals in South Korea. 'Endangered' means these bears could disappear from Earth if something is not done to save them. The South Korean government has imported 27 Asiatic black bear cubs from Russia and North Korea and released them into the Jirisan National Park to increase the number of these big, beautiful animals in the country.

Forest and wildlife experts have also seen Asiatic black bears in the Seoraksan Mountains in the northeastern part of South Korea.

Siberian musk deer — You can see these small deer in the Jeollanam and Gangwon provinces of South Korea. Their small size helps these pretty deer hide from their predators behind rocks and allows them run quickly.

Minke whale — The common minke whale is a sub-species of baleen whales. Its meat is considered to be very delicious. Sadly, because of this, the population of the common minke whale is reducing rapidly. Illegal hunting of the common minke whale is taken very seriously in my country, and the coast guards have arrested many poachers. Poachers are illegal hunters who hunt endangered and protected animals.

Here are some interesting facts about the common minke whale:
They are one of the smallest whales in the world. They grow to about 22-24 feet in length and weigh up to 14 tons. They use their baleen plates to filter out the food from the water they drink. They eat small fish like sardines and herring, small crustaceans like crabs, and squids.

They swim slowly during their feeding time and swim quickly when they feel threatened. That's easy to understand, isn't it?
Minke whales can make loud song-like sounds that can be heard nearly 2 miles away.

Northern fur seal — You can find the northern fur seals in the East Sea between Korea and Japan. Just to jog your memory, East Sea is the same body of water that Japan refers to as the Sea of Japan. Northern fur seals are born black but become gray in 4 months after their birth.

Do you know that the northern fur seals are solitary feeders and use their whiskers to smell and locate food even in murky waters?

Korean Magpie – is the national bird of South Korea. We Koreans believe that when this cute little bird chirps at our doorstep, then an unexpected visitor will come home. And the best part of this belief is that this unexpected visitor will bring good luck!

Here are some fun facts about these little birds:

- They eat flies, insects, and fruits too.
- The call of the Korean magpie sounds like 'yak' or 'mag'!
- They are mostly black with some white in the tail area, feathers, and the breast region. If you look closely, these birds have shades of blue-green, too.
- The Korean magpie belongs to the crow family.

Korean water deer – One of the most significant differences between Korean water deer and the other classes of deer, including the Chinese water deer, is that they have tusks instead of antlers.

They have long and elegant necks and their front legs are shorter than the rear legs which makes them look like they are carrying their shoulders very high.

As the name already indicates, they live close to rivers. They are excellent swimmers and prefer to move in water rather than on land. They eat twigs, grass, berries, and other forms of vegetation.

Asian badger – These small creatures belong to the same family as otters and weasels. They live in open areas of deciduous and coniferous

What are the nests of Asian badgers called?

1. Dens
2. Nests
3. Setts

Answer: (3) Setts; the badgers burrow them under the ground)

What is the name given to animals that eat plants instead of meat?

1. Carnivore
2. Herbivore
3. Omnivore

Answer: (2) Herbivore

Korean Crevice Salamander – The Korean crevice salamander dwells under rocks in limestone forest areas of the Korean peninsula, and is the only lungless salamander known from Asia. Discovered in Daejeon in 2005, the species is considered locally common, and reasonably widespread, but has not been well studied in the field. Therefore, its natural history, population dynamics and reproductive behavior remain unknown.

Native Plants of South Korea

> Can you recall the national flower of South Korea?
>
> 1. The Mugunghwa
> 2. The White Rose
> 3. The Violets
>
> Answer: (1) The Mugunghwa

Mugunghwa flower — This special flower was treasured by the Koreans even in ancient times as a 'Blossom from Heaven.' In fact, the Shilla Kingdom called itself the 'Country of the Mugunghwa' or Geunhwahyang. Even the Chinese referred to Korea as 'The Land of Wise People Where the Mugunghwa Flower Blooms.'

This flower is a Korean symbol used in all government badges, decorations, national organizations, etc.

Korean red pine — The Korean red pine holds special meaning in the hearts of the Koreans. This tree represents virtue, longevity, honor, wisdom, and strength. Many Koreans pray to certain pine trees that they believe are sacred.

Pine branches are left on the doors when babies are born as a way of congratulating the new parents. Also, the pine needles are used as ingredients in many dishes, especially Korean teas. There is a pine tree whose wood was used to make the roof of the oldest building in Korea that still stands in Mount Bukhan. We call this tree as sol-namu, which translates to 'the best tree.' This oldest surviving wooden building is Geukrakjeon, or the Nirvana Hall, which was built in the times of the Koryo Dynasty.

Camphor Tree — belongs to the laurel family. The twigs, roots, and leaves of this tree emit the smell of camphor. The fruits of the camphor trees are consumed by many birds and animals. The leaves of this tree are used as a spice, and the roots are made into a kind of tea. Both are known to have excellent medicinal value.

Three-Flowered Maple — In the autumn season, the leaves of this tree change beautifully from yellow to orange to red creating a burst of colors.

CHAPTER 6
FAMOUS PEOPLE FROM SOUTH KOREA

King Sejong's Statue in Seoul, South Korea

King Sejong the Great — Do you recall his name? He was the one who developed Hangul, the Korean alphabet and writing system to promote literacy among common people. Before Hangul, Chinese script was widely used in Korea, but due to its complexity, it was difficult to teach it to the lower class. In comparison, Hangul can typically be learned in a few hours of study!

Even today, Hangul Day is celebrated to remember and honor this king and his writing system. He also encouraged inventors, artists, and people in literature. His reign is known for technological and innovative progress. Also, he had a strong defense force which kept Korea safe from foreign invasions.

King Gwanggaeto the Great — He was part of the Koguryo Kingdom. Nearly two-thirds of Korea along with parts of Mongolia and Manchuria were part of the Koguryo Kingdom during his rule. The Koguryo Kingdom became very famous in East Asia under his rule. We know about this great king from a stone slab called Gwanggaeto Stele on which all his achievements were engraved.

Jinheung of Silla — He was a king of the Shilla Kingdom, was known for his military and diplomatic powers, and because of these he was able to extend and expand the Shilla Kingdom. Using his powers and diplomacy, he was able to attack both the Koguryo and the Pekche territories and make them part of the Shilla Kingdom.

Seongdok of Silla — He was another king of the Shilla Kingdom. By the time he came to power, nearly the entire southern part of Korea was unified under the control of the Shilla. There was peace and prosperity during this king's rule, and a lot of progress in the field of art and literature was made then.

Therefore, for any Korean king to get the word 'great' added to his name, he had to do one or more of the following: Expand his territories using military, diplomacy, or provide a rule of stability where art and literature flourished.

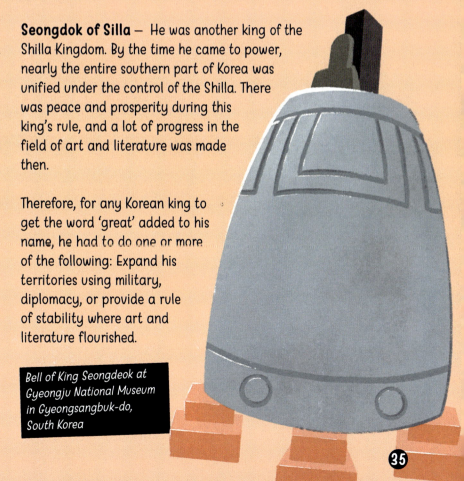
Bell of King Seongdeok at Gyeongju National Museum in Gyeongsangbuk-do, South Korea

Famous People in the Modern Period

Ban Ki-Moon — He is a former secretary-general of the United Nations, born on June 13, 1944. As a teenager, he won an essay competition organized by the Red Cross. The prize was a trip to the US where he met John F. Kennedy. This meeting made him decide that he wanted to become a diplomat. Ban Ki-Moon was the 8th United Nations secretary-general and was appointed for a second term as well in 2011. He earned the nickname 'The Bureaucrat' for his great diplomatic skills. He spread awareness about the importance and effects of global warming across the globe.

> What does a diplomat do?
> 1. Keep good relations between countries and people
> 2. Write books and novels.
> 3. Develop computer software
>
> Answer: (1) Keep good relations between countries and people.

Bang Jeong-hwan — He wrote books for children and helped setting up Children's Day in Korea. In Korea, he is known as the father of children's literature. I think South Korea is one of the very few countries which declares Children's Day as a national holiday!

He believed that children should be respected as much as adults. He translated many books into the Korean language, and the most popular translation work he did was the fairy tales of Hans Christian Andersen. He also set up a lot of organizations for children welfare.

Psy — is a South Korean songwriter, record producer, rapper, and singer who popularized the hit single "Gangnam Style" in 2012. In December of the same year, it became the first video to hit 1 billion views on Youtube.

During his popularity, U.N. Secretary General Ban Ki-moon even expressed his interest in meeting with Psy, believing that his music and influence could be an instrument to reduce conflict and intolerance.

In 2013, A 'Gangnam Style Horse Dancing Stage' was put up in Seoul's Gangnam district to pay tribute to kpop artist Psy.

Song Il-Gook — He is a famous South Korean actor who is best known for his role in drama series 'Jumong', a fictional retelling of King Dongmyeong's life in the Goguryeo period. Aside from being an actor, he is also a model, a triathlete, and a sketch artist. The state of Hawaii has a day named after him. Yes, March 21 is called 'Song Il-gook Day' in Hawaii.

Park Ji-Sung — He is a South Korean soccer player, fondly nicknamed 'Three Lungs Park'. His soccer-playing talent was recognized early on, and he played for his elementary school.

Very soon, he was recognized as one of the brightest stars in the field of South Korean soccer. He played for Manchester United as a midfielder from 2005-2012 and was named the captain of the South Korean football team in 2010.

Kim Yuna — is a famous figure skater from South Korea. She started skating from the time she was five years old. Her coach told her mother then that her body and muscles were naturally made for figure skating.
She was born in Bucheon in the Gyeonggi Province in 1990 and moved to Gunpo in 1996 when she was six years old.

The correct spelling of her name is Kim Yeona. But, she wanted her name to be spelled as Yun-a in her passport. However, the official at the passport office made a mistake and spelled her name as Yu-na. You see, there is a very small difference between the way Yun-a and Yu-na are written in the Korean language.

Kim Yuna is the youngest skater to have won the senior title at the South Korean Figure Skating Championships. Her skating music and other favorite songs of Kim Yuna were put together into a music album titled, Yuna Kim ~ Fairy on ICE ~ Skating Music.

> She suffered from a serious injury in 2006 and was healed by a Roman Catholic doctor.
>
> Her Catholic name is Stella Maris.

Famous Comanies of South Korea

The Samsung Group – Samsung started its journey way back in 1938. The name Samsung comes from two Korean words namely sam (which means three) and sung (which means) stars. Samsung, therefore, means three stars which represent powerful, big, and numerous.

Can you believe it?! Samsung started as a noodle making company with 40 staff. Today, it is one of the largest global companies in the world with nearly 500,000 employees. The Samsung Group has businesses in electronics, mobiles, ship-building, construction, even financial services.

Did you know what Samsung's first business was?

1. Electronics
2. Mobiles
3. Noodle making

Answer: (3) Noodle making

LG Electronics – The main purpose of setting up this company was to make sure that Koreans could buy locally made electronics goods like radio, TV, refrigerator, air conditioners, washing machines, etc.

The name LG came about in 1995 when GoldStar merged with Lak-Hui Chemical to form Lucky-GoldStar which become LG. Today, electronic items from LG are popular all over the world. We Koreans are very proud of all these multinational companies that successfully became household names all over the world.

Hyundai Motors – Did you know that Hyundai in Korean translates to 'Modernity?'

Have you seen the Hyundai H badge? It is actually a stylized form of two people who are shaking hands. One person is the company staff, and the other person is the customer. The handshake stands for trust and satisfaction for the customer. And the circle around the H badge means Hyundai wants to do this for the entire world.

Also, Hyundai makes its own steel for manufacturing its cars. It does not buy steel from any other seller. Hyundai's Ulsan factory is one of the largest factories in the world, covering more than 54-million square foot of space.

CHAPTER 7
IMPORTANT CITIES AND MAJOR ATTRACTIONS

In this section, I will tell you about some of the top cities of South Korea and the main attractions there.

Seoul

As you already know by now, Seoul is the capital of South Korea. It has a population of over 10 million, so it is known as a megacity. Seoul is the center of South Korea's politics, economy, and culture. Seoul was known by different names right through its history. Seoul itself comes from the Korean word Seoraneol, which translates to 'Capital City.'

Seoul was founded in 18 B.C. by the Pekche Kingdom. During the Japanese occupation, Seoul was called Gyeongseong, but when Korea gained independence from Japan in 1945, it was renamed Seoul. Considering that Seoul has an old history, it is home to many beautiful, historic monuments and buildings many of which are UNESCO World Heritage Sites.

In which year did Seoul host the Olympics Games?

1. 1994
2. 1998
3. 2002

Answer: (3) 2002

The Changdeokgung Palace Complex

It is one of the five grand palaces of South Korea, the other four being Gyeongbokgung, Deoksugung, Gyeonghuigung, and Changgyunggung. The construction started in 1405 and completed in 1412. Changdeokgung is Korean for 'The Palace of Prospering Virtue'.

There are numerous buildings within the palace which also an enjoyable park for kids and families. Also, the National Palace Museum and the National Folk Museum are housed here.

The Jongmyo Shrine — This Confucian shrine is the oldest surviving shrine in South Korea. You can see memorial tablets and stone slabs about the various Choson kings and queens right from the 14th century.

An important thing to remember when you are visiting any shrine is not to walk on the central path leading to the main shrine because that path is for the spirits of the shrine. Visitors are also expected to observe silence during visits.

Lotte World — Kids cannot miss out this place. It has a huge indoor theme park, an artificial island which is connected through a monorail, an outdoor amusement park, movie theaters, sports facilities, and many more fun things to see and do.

Lotte World is open all year long without any holiday closings!

Busan

Busan, earlier written as Pusan, is the largest port city in South Korea, and is located on the southeastern tip of the Korean peninsula. The population of Busan is about 3.5 million.

Busan played an important role during the Korean War because it was one of the last bastions of power held by the South Koreans. During the Korean War, Busan was the provisional capital of South Korea. Some of the places of interest in Busan are:

Busan Tower — Built in 1973, the tower is a 120m (about 394 ft) located in Yongdusan Park.

Unlike other towers in South Korea, Busan Tower doesn't have any transmitter and is used solely for leisure and entertainment.

It is practically an observation deck for those who want to enjoy a panoramic view of Busan. The tower is open from 10am to 11pm so people can visit late in the afternoon to enjoy the sunset and night lights.

Gamcheon Culture Village — Every home in this cultural village in Busan is painted in an artistic way making the whole place look like one big piece of art. Also, the cute little streets within the village lead you to many interesting art studios and other fun places you can see.

The Village began as a shanty town in the 1950's and was built by Korean War refugees.

In 2009, the Ministry of Culture, Sports, and Tourism called on artists to decorate the village. With their brightly painted houses, the village has been reborn as Busan's most colorful and artistic spot and has been dubbed as Machu Pichu of Busan.

Haeundae Beach — One of the most popular beaches in South Korea. It is also one of the most expensive ones outside Seoul.

Right in the center of this beautiful beach is a Folk Square where you can play a lot of traditional Korean games like seesaw jumping, Korean wrestling, tug-of-war, and arrow-throwing.

Incheon

This city is located in the northwestern part of South Korea and borders Seoul to the east. This port-city with a population of around 3 million is the third most populated city in my country. Being a port city, it is also one of the largest maritime hubs in Asia.

Incheon translates to 'Kind River' or 'Wise River'. The most famous landmark of Incheon Metropolitan City is its modern international airport. In 2007, Incheon has declared itself an "English City," and advocated the "Incheon Free English Zone" program to make the city proficient in English and thus improve the city's economy.

Sunset in Ganghwa Island, Incheon.

Gangwhwa Island — This island is separated from mainland Incheon by a little channel and is a prehistoric burial ground. The Koryo Royal family escaped to this island when the Mongols invaded Korea in the 13th century. They repelled Mongolian attacks for 39 years from the island of Ganghwa.

Historical Monuments and Museums — As Incheon is an important part of Korean history, you will see multiple monuments and museums here. Some of them include Modern Architecture Museum and the Incheon Landing Operation Memorial Hall.

Daegu

Also spelled as Taegu, Daegu is one of the largest cities in South Korea along with Seoul, Incheon, and Busan. Daegu was called the 'City of Apples and Beauties' because it was believed that the beautiful ladies here got their beauty from eating the wonderful apples grown in this area.

Today, Daegu is South Korea's biggest producer of glasses and textiles. Multiple historical and natural museums are located in Daegu. Some of the major attractions in the city are the Wolgok History Museum, Daegu Arts Center, Haengso Museum of Keimyung University and more!

The Palgongsan Mountain Mount Palgongsan is located in the northeastern part of Daegu and houses the Palgongsan national park and a number of natural treasures and cultural heritage sites dating back from the Silla period. You can take walks in the park or ride the Palgongsan Cable Car which takes you from the base of Mount Palgongsan to a height of 800 meters where you can see the sky garden and Naenggol forest park.

Daejeon

Daejeon or Taejon hasa population of over 1.5 million. Daejeon is located in the central part of South Korea. You can reach Seoul in 50 minutes from Daejeon if you travel by the KTX high-speed train.

The expansion of the city began in the 1900s when the Seoul-Busan railway line was built by the Japanese. Daejeon is a hub of science and technology, thanks to Daedok Science Town. In fact, it has got the nickname 'Korea's Silicon Valley.'

Ppuri Park – Called as the Root Park, the Ppuri Park is unique because it traces the history of different family surnames in Korea. There are numerous stone sculptures here containing historical descriptions of the various Korean family names. The family name Kim is the most common one in Korea.

Daejeon Expo Science Park
This park was built to raise awareness about science and technology. Many science-based buildings are here including Advanced Science & Technology Center, National Science Museum of Korea, Earthscape, Technopia, Visions of Korea pavilions, and Starquest.

Currency Museum of Korea
This museum is the first to showcase the history and facts about the currencies of Korea. Over 120,000 coins including some from the Choson Kingdom are on display.

Jeju City

Jeju City is the capital of Jejudo Island, one of the 9 provinces of South Korea. It has some breathtaking beaches, beautiful cliffs, and warm, welcoming people.

> Can you guess the nickname of Jeju Island?
> 1. Hawaii of the East
> 2. San Francisco of the East
> 3. Venice of the East
>
> Answer: (1) Hawaii of the East

The Tewoo Beach — Very close to downtown Jeju, it is easy to reach Tewoo Beach. You can rent boats, go fishing, explore the lighthouses in the area, and take a walk along the pine trees. Spending a day on this beach is a lot of fun.

Museums — There are many unusual museums to see in Jeju including the Teddy Bear Museum, the Trick Eye Museum (an interactive place where paintings are created using 3D techniques), and the Haenyeo Museum.

Hiking Trails — There are many hiking trails that almost cover the entire island of Jeju. There is a special UNESCO-designated trail that takes you through 9 different peaks in Jeju.

Abalone is the most expensive seafood here, and these sea creatures are caught by specially-trained lady divers called haenyeo.

Gwangju

Gwangju, also spelled as Kwangju, is situated in southwest South Korea. This old city borders the mountainous region of the South Cholla Province.

People believe it was founded in 57 B.C. and since then has been the center of trade and commerce in Korea. Today, there are multiple industries in Gwangju including cotton textiles, rice mills, telecom industries, and breweries.

Let me tell you about some of my favorite attractions in Gwangju.

Boseong Tea Fields — Beautiful, lush green tea gardens welcome you here. You can learn a lot about Korean culture by interacting with the locals in this place. There are many gorgeous spots, which will give you amazing photoshoot opportunities. Your friends back home will also want to come and visit Korea.

Daewonsa Temple — This beautiful temple is dedicated to Tibetan Buddhism. You can view and experience the beauty of nature in this temple. There are wooded paths, bubbling streams, and beautiful mountain trails.

Suwon

In the times of the Three Kingdoms, the area in and around modern-day Suwon was called Maehol-gun. Here are some interesting places in Suwon City:

The Hwaesong Fortress — The wall that surrounds the Suwon City is called the Hwaseong Fortress. This fortress was built by King Jeongjo of Choson Dynasty to try and shift the capital of Korea to Suwon.

Hwaseong is the venue of several events in the city such as Martial Arts Performances and the Royal Guards Ceremony. So you might even get to experience one when you visit the city.

The Hwaseong Haenggung Palace — This palace was used by many kings as a temporary holiday and relaxation place. In fact, King Jeongjo would come here very often to escape from the hustle-bustle of his Seoul palace. Today, there are reenactment shows which feature sword fights.

Goyang-si

Located to the north of Seoul, the best part of this beautiful city is that it is wonderfully combined with the rural areas so you can experience both the urban and the village life of Goyang-si. Here are some of the major attractions in this city:

Korea International Exhibition Center or KINTEX
This place is the biggest exhibit area in Korea with multiple conference rooms and 10 main exhibition halls. Goyang city has become a major international exhibition center. KINTEX offers a great business environment, world-class facilities, and professional services to companies that come here to exhibit their services and products.

Lake Park — Opened on May 14, 1996, Lake Park is a man-made lake surrounded by with beautiful parks. You can enjoy the Musical Fountain too inside this park.

Baedagol Theme Park — This unique park is dedicated to ecological balance and environmental preservation. In this place, you can see and experience ancient handicrafts and arts. There are activities that allow you to make carp necklaces and other art pieces.

Ulsan

Ulsan is located in the southeastern part of South Korea. This highly urbanized city had humble origins as a fishing port.

> Can you recall the company that has one of the biggest factories here?
>
> 1. Hyundai
> 2. LG Electronics
> 3. Samsung
>
> Answer: (1.) Hyundai

Hyundai also operates the largest shipyard in Ulsan. The public transport system in Ulsan is world-class, and the KTX high-speed train network extends to this city, too. Thanks to this, Ulsan can be reached from Seoul in just 2 hours.

The Taehwa River Grand Park — This beautiful trekking place has a river that flows right through the center of the city and empties into Ulsan Bay, which is connected to the East Sea.

You can start from the Taehwa Bridge, walk down to the bamboo forest, then take the main road back where you are likely to see a festival or performance.

Seonam Lake Park — This lake park was once an industrial reservoir. Today, there are walking paths right around the lake. As you walk here, you can see miniature cathedrals and churches. They are tiny buildings, but you can enter them and pray! During springtime, this lake park is full of beautiful cherry blossoms.

Daewangam Park — A pine forest in this park allows you a breath of fresh air right in the middle of an urban town. This park also provides great ocean views and scenes of the port.

Conclusion

I hope you enjoyed the tour across my beautiful country of South Korea as much as I enjoyed it. I thought it would be a great idea to finish our trip across South Korea with a simple quiz. So, here goes:

When did North Korea attack South Korea?
1. 1945
2. 1931
3. 1950

Answer: (3) 1950

What is the national sport of South Korea?
1. Tennis
2. Basketball
3. Tae Kwon Do

Answer: (3) Tae Kwon Do

What is the traditional Korean dress called?
1. Kimono
2. Hanbok
3. Salwar

Answer: (2) Hanbok

What is kimchi?
1. Pickled vegetables; mostly cabbage
2. A meat dish
3. A drink

Answer: (1) Pickled vegetables

Which country helped South Korea in the Korean War?
1. Russia
2. Japan
3. The USA

(Answer: (3) The USA

What is the South Korean flag called in the Korean language?
1. Keungukki
2. Minjuki
3. Taegukki

Answer: (3) Taegukki

Can you recall the most common Korean surname?
1. Jim
2. Lim
3. Kim

Answer: (3) Kim

Which city in Korea hosted the 2002 Olympic Games?
1. Seoul
2. Ulsan
3. Busan

Answer: (1) Seoul

What does Gangnam refer to in the popular song of Psy 'Gangnam Style?'
1. A way to eat to kimchi
2. A Korean dance
3. A district in Seoul

Answer: (3) A district in Seoul

What kind of government exists in South Korea today?
1. Monarchy
2. Democracy
3. Communist

(Answer: (2) Democracy

*I have thoroughly enjoyed this journey through France with you.
Feel free to visit us at www.dinobibi.com and check out our other titles!*

Dinobibi Travel for Kids

Dinobibi History for Kids

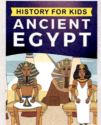 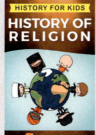 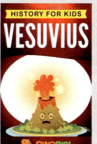  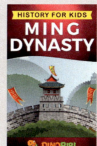
   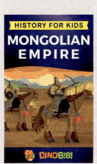 

Made in the USA
Las Vegas, NV
24 March 2024